Original title:
Yuletide Dreams and Winter Gleams

Copyright © 2024 Creative Arts Management OÜ
All rights reserved.

Author: Miriam Kensington
ISBN HARDBACK: 978-9916-90-946-1
ISBN PAPERBACK: 978-9916-90-947-8

The Tenderness of Quiet Snowfall

When snowflakes fall, they tiptoe light,
Pretending all the world's just right.
They land on noses, dogs, and cars,
Transforming rooftops into bars.

The snowmen grin with carrot noses,
They scheme and giggle, striking poses.
With sticks for arms, they wave and shout,
While children take their snowball route.

The cat looks out, all wide-eyed,
Thinking, 'What's this fluffy slide?'
He pounces out but swiftly slips,
In snow, he hops with goofy flips!

The world's a canvas, white and bright,
Where everyone sheds their serious plight.
In silence falls the playful snow,
Making merry hearts aglow.

Frosted Hues and Midnight Blues

The snowflakes dance and prance about,
Each one refuses to let out a shout.
A snowman's carrot may soon get snatched,
The local birds, they're truly unmatched.

With frosted hues that sparkle so bright,
They claim that winter is quite a delight.
But shoveling snow is no easy feat,
Watch out for that slip; don't land on your seat!

Twinkling Lanterns on Silent Streets

The lanterns flicker, casting a glow,
A raccoon's out, putting on quite a show.
He scales the trash can, what a display,
Even the cats are like, 'Not today!'

Silent streets and the air, crisp and cold,
Where stories of mischief are always told.
A dog in a sweater, bustling with pride,
Barks at the moon, 'I'm coming outside!'

The Warmth Beneath Icicles

Icicles hang like swords from above,
Dreaming of summer and sunshine we love.
They drip drop, drip, in a rhythmic tune,
Reminding us spring is coming quite soon.

Beneath them, warmth finds a sneaky way,
Hot cocoa waits at the end of the day.
But watch your step; that puddle's a trap,
One splash and you'll spill that hot chocolate lap!

A Tapestry of Quiet Nights

The stars are out, like jewels on a thread,
Knitting dreams in the sky, overhead.
A cat on a fence, acting all smug,
Claims this quiet night is its favorite drug.

A tapestry woven of giggles and sighs,
As neighbors warm up with cookies and pies.
The laughter drifts out through the window panes,
While outside, snowflakes nail a chill that remains!

Silent Snowfall Serenade

Snowflakes dance and spin so bright,
They tickle noses, what a sight!
Squirrels slip, then they zoom,
On icy paths, they find their zoom.

Silent nights, the world does freeze,
While penguins wear their coats with ease.
Hot cocoa dreams in fuzzy socks,
As winter joy around us blocks.

Glimmers of Frosted Wishes

Frosty windows, magic views,
Kids making snowmen with cartoon shoes.
Elves wrapped in blankets, cozy and tight,
Share giggles and snacks by candlelight.

Candies sparkle, sweet delight,
The gingerbread men begin to fight.
All the wishes wrapped in bows,
Will melt away with summer's throes.

Wreathed in White Wonders

Fluffy hats on heads, oh dear,
Can't feel my ears, winter's here!
Snowball fights erupt with glee,
Though someone just hit a tree!

Icicles dangling, quite the sight,
A frozen sword; it's pure delight.
Slipping and sliding, shouts prevail,
As laughter echoes down the trail.

Echoes of the Season's Glow

Winter's here with frosty air,
Running to catch snowflakes fair.
Hot soup served with cheeky grins,
As snowball battles spark with wins.

Chilly nights and warm hearth's cheer,
Singing songs that all can hear.
Shimmering lights on every street,
Winter magic, oh so sweet!

Cozy Corners and Whispered Secrets

In cozy corners where we hide,
Whispers flow, our hearts collide.
The cat's the queen; she's got the chair,
While crumbs dance free without a care.

A sock starts talking, what a surprise!
It tells the tales of our alibis.
The coffee's strong, the cookies sweet,
In this little den, we find our beat.

The clock ticks loud, a comedy show,
Time doesn't count; it's nice to go slow.
We laugh at dreams that pop like balloons,
In our cozy corner, we're silly cartoons.

Illusions of Frost on Window Panes

Frosty patterns twist and twirl,
Are they art or just a swirl?
A snowman winks, we start to sing,
As winter's chill makes our hearts fling.

The ice on glass is quite a tease,
It shows us shapes, like frozen cheese.
Snowflakes giggle as they dance down,
Making white blankets for every town.

But somehow, on the hot cocoa spree,
We spill it all, oh dear, oh me!
Still, laughter rises, hot like steam,
In our frosty world, we live the dream.

The Magic of Glimmering Pines

In evergreen forests, lights blink and glow,
Whispers of magic in the fresh snow.
A squirrel pirouettes, what a sight!
With acorns for shoes, he dances all night.

Fairy lights draped on every tree,
The pine smells like home, wild and free.
As owls hoot out their nightly song,
We join in chorus; we can't go wrong.

With mugs held high, we toast to the stars,
The trees sway gently; they've come from Mars.
Laughter and joy are in the air,
Under groaning branches, we find our flair.

Embracing the Chill with Heartfelt Cheer

The chilly breeze gives us the shivers,
But laughter warms; it's what delivers.
Bundled up like a marshmallow treat,
We stomp in snow with frosty feet.

Sledding down hills is quite the show,
With every bump, we scream, "Whee! Go!"
A snowball flies, oh what a blast,
A face full of snow, a cold, slick cast.

We gather round with stories to share,
Hot chocolate spills, but we don't care.
So here's to the chill and heartfelt cheer,
In winter's embrace, we end the year.

Shivering Shadows and Golden Dreams

In the chilly night, shadows creep,
Dreams are golden, yet lost in sleep.
Frosty whispers dance on the breeze,
Chasing after warmth, if you please.

Giggles and shivers, a strange delight,
With marshmallows melting, oh what a sight!
Shadows that shiver with cold and glee,
Join in the laughter, come play with me.

But beware the chill that's lurking near,
It tickles your toes and nips at your ear.
Lost in the dreams of a sugary treat,
Waking to find no socks on your feet!

So grab a blanket, let's snuggle tight,
In shivering shadows, we'll giggle all night.
With dreams of hot cocoa to melt the frost,
Together we'll warm up, never lost!

Flickering Flames of Holiday Spirit

The flickering flames dance in delight,
Candles sing songs on this chilly night.
With cookies and cocoa, we spread the cheer,
Who knew holiday spirit would come with a beer?

Snowflakes that twirl in the festive air,
Tangled in lights, the trees look quite rare.
Gingerbread houses, oh what a sight,
Who knew icing could start an epic fight?

Stockings a-hanging, with prizes that gleam,
The dog steals the turkey—it's part of the scheme.
Merry chaos, it's holiday bliss,
Let's not forget that awkward family kiss!

So gather around, let's share some laughs,
With flickering flames, we'll craft our own paths.
With spirits aglow and hearts full of cheer,
May your holidays be wild, like that one aunt's beer!

The Realm of Frosted Fantasies

In a realm of frost where the snowmen dwell,
They tell funny tales with a jolly yell.
Snowballs are tossed with laughter and cheer,
And snowflakes giggle when they touch your ear.

Penguins in bowties slide down the hills,
Making snow angels, oh what a thrill!
With frosted cupcakes that sparkle and shine,
Who knew snow frosting could taste so divine?

Chubby reindeer practicing their prance,
Gliding through snow, they take quite a chance.
With sleigh bells ringing, the spirit is grand,
Together we dance in this frosty wonderland.

So come join the fun in this frosted tour,
Where laughter and joy are always in store.
With fanciful dreams and a snowman parade,
In this magical realm, let worries fade!

Starlit Strolls Under the Moon's Gaze

Under a blanket of twinkling stars,
We wander in dreams, forgetting our cars.
The moon's playful wink says, 'Come take a walk!'
But watch for the dog—it's a sneaky old hawk!

With laughter and songs echoing bright,
Beneath the soft glow of the silvery light.
Holding ice cream cones, they start to drip,
Suddenly, a duck joins the fun with a quip!

Careful, don't trip on that stray little cat,
Who's curled up and snoozing, all cozy and fat.
We step over puddles, we skip with delight,
While pondering if Reynolds can find a rare bite.

So here's to the nights that make spirits soar,
With starlit strolls and dreams to explore.
Let's dance under stars, let's twirl and twine,
In this whimsical journey, your heart will align!

Soft Footfalls on Snowy Paths

In boots so big, I trudge along,
Each step a clumsy, snowy song.
The snowflakes giggle, swirl, and dance,
While I just hope to avoid a prance.

My nose is red, my cheeks are bright,
I'm looking quite a silly sight.
The snowman grins, his hat askew,
While I just wobble, like a zoo!

The icy wind gives me a shove,
I tumble hard, but still I love.
Snowball fights with all my crew,
But watch out! You know I'll target you!

With frosty breath, I shout with glee,
The world's a snowy jubilee.
Soft footfalls, oh what a delight,
Let's twirl and spin in winter's light!

Twilight Musings on a Frosted Eve

The twilight dances, glows so bright,
With frosted trees, what a sight!
I sip my cocoa, feeling grand,
But my marshmallow's made a stand.

It floats so high, it's quite the tease,
I think it's plotting, if you please.
Will it dive in, or float away?
Marshmallow drama? What a play!

The snowflakes start a downward race,
While I'm just trying to keep pace.
They whisper secrets, soft and small,
While I just slip and trip and fall!

Yet in this frosty, snowy dream,
Life's just a silly, joyful theme.
Twilight musings, laughs in store,
Let's dance and tumble, who could want more?

Dreamy Nights Under the Snowy Canopy

The skies above, they twinkle bright,
As fluffy snowflakes kiss goodnight.
I snuggle up, my blanket tight,
But snores escape, oh what a fright!

The dreamland whispers, soft and sweet,
But once again, I miss my seat.
I dream of sledding, fast and wild,
And wake up tangled, just a child!

A frosty moon, my pillow friend,
It glows with laughter, no end.
Snowy canopy, oh so fun,
Get ready world, I'm on the run!

With dreams of snowmen, snowball fights,
My heart leaps up on winter nights.
So cozy here, under the glow,
Let's dream of laughter, as we go!

Echoes of Frosted Whispers

The whispers of frost dance through the air,
Echoes of giggles, with frosty flair.
Sipping hot chocolate, I trip and slip,
Yet laughter erupts, can't help but zip!

With the snowflakes gracing my nose,
I join the dance, in winter's pose.
But oh! I'm caught in a snowflake snare,
A frosty embrace, oh what a dare!

The trees, they chuckle, their branches sway,
As snowmen gossip and play all day.
With frosted whispers shared with glee,
Winter's a carnival, come join me!

And as I prance through this snowy tale,
I trip once more, but I won't bail.
The echoes of laughter fill the night,
In frosted whispers, everything's right!

The Warmth of Kindled Fires

In blankets piled high, we sit tight,
With marshmallows roasting, oh what a sight!
The crackling sound is quite the cheer,
But who smuggled in all this gooey smear?

We laugh as one jumps and nearly falls,
The dog steals a snack, he barely appalls.
Hot chocolate spills on the carpeted floor,
Now it's a party, who could ask for more?

As shadows dance on the wall with flair,
Uncle Joe's jokes bring us gasps for air.
With each punchline, even Grandma blinks,
We realize too, the cat also drinks!

So here we are, in a fiery glow,
With laughter and sweets, we steal the show.
When winter's cold knocks on our door,
A warm fire's glow always offers more.

Lanterns in the Snowlight

Hanging lanterns light up the way,
They flicker and shimmer in cold dismay.
But when one falls with a cheeky thump,
We all jump back in a snowy lump!

Bob's stuck inside with that awful hat,
Looking like something that just fell flat.
His snowman compadre, a lopsided gnome,
Taught us all that we should just stay home.

Yet out we trudge with our hearts aglow,
Feeding the squirrels as they watch the show.
"Why are you throwing those nuts at me?"
"Because we think you look adorable, you see!"

As lanterns sway, we sing out loud,
In the frigid air, we feel so proud.
With laughter and frosty breath in sync,
We'll warm our hearts before we sink!

Echoes of Laughter Through Winter's Veil

In the hush of snow, whispers arise,
Laughter echoes beneath frosty skies.
With snowballs flying, the chaos begins,
And who just tripped? Oh, let the fun spin!

We roll giant snowmen with quite the style,
Their carrot noses make us all smile.
But one cheeky fellow, a snowman unfit,
Is just a tall pile with a dog sit!

Through frosted trees, we hear merry sounds,
As kids chase the cat while the neighbor bounds.
The air blasts with giggles, no room for gloom,
Even the snowflakes seem to twirl and zoom!

So let winter come with its chilly embrace,
For laughter's the fire we all can chase.
Through winter's veil, we smile and cheer,
Holding memories dear, year after year.

A Symphony of Snowflakes Falling

A symphony plays as snowflakes descend,
Glittering notes that jingle and blend.
Each flake has a story, oh what a feat,
They twirl and they dance, what a frosty treat!

Oh look at that one, it's shaped like a star,
While another looks like a mustached czar.
There's one falling gently, too shy to land,
It just swirls around like a tiny band!

The snowmen are camping, their eyebrows of ice,
Next to our snowball piles, oh, how nice!
Yet suddenly splat! A rogue ball flies through,
And giggles erupt from a *very* chill crew!

So gather your mittens, cheer, and don't fret,
In this chilly game, there's no room for regret.
When winter's moon glows on this delight,
It's a symphony played under stars so bright!

Gleaming Trails of Silver Light

In the night, the stars do shine,
Cats chase tails, a sight divine.
The moon grins with a wink so sly,
While owls hoot a bedtime sigh.

Fairies dance on soft moonbeams,
Trading secrets, sharing dreams.
A raccoon steals a midnight snack,
While whispers float, no fear of lack.

Frogs in tuxedos croak a tune,
As crickets strum beneath the moon.
A firefly's glow, a twinkling spark,
Illuminates the playful dark.

A Dance of Shadows and Stars

Ghosts in pajamas start to sway,
Booing softly in a playful way.
The pumpkins roll, a grinning crew,
While bats breakdance, just for you.

Witches brew some fizzy drinks,
With eyeballs floating, what one thinks!
Goblins giggle, doing the twist,
In this haunted, foggy mist.

A shadow jumped and gave a shout,
"Who wants to dance? Come on out!"
With all these ghouls, oh what a sight,
It's a party under starry light!

Mistletoe Kisses and Pine-Scented Wishes

Beneath the mistletoe, a festive cheer,
A cat stole kisses and left with a sneer.
The dog joined in with a slobbery grin,
While Grandma danced, her face in a spin.

Elves on shelves, they share the fun,
Sneaking cookies after everyone.
The tree's all tangled, lights gone wild,
And Cousin Eddie is still a child.

Socks stuffed full of playful things,
Like rubber ducks and paper rings.
Pine-scented wishes float in the air,
A holiday jolly, without a care!

The Lullaby of Chilly Winds

When winter whispers, frosty and bright,
The squirrels snuggle, ready for night.
The snowflakes giggle, falling down,
While penguins waddle, wearing a crown.

Frosty's hat has taken flight,
On a chilly breeze, a comical sight.
The fireplace crackles, so warm and snug,
While the cat's dreaming of a plump bug.

Icicles dangle like a toothy grin,
While children laugh, bundled up in skin.
The chilly winds sing a soft refrain,
Of cozy cuddles and snowball gain.

The Quiet Dance of Winter Light

In the fridge, the pickles sway,
The leftover turkey steals the day.
Icicles hang like frozen spears,
While snowmen laugh and toast with beers.

The sun peeks out, shy and bright,
While squirrels hold a snowball fight.
Flakes of joy swirl in the air,
As hot cocoa spills without a care.

Frosty smiles on windows cling,
While carolers annoy the cats that sing.
The holiday lights start to twinkle,
A dance-off for stars as they sprinkle.

Mistletoe Dreams Beneath the Boughs

Under boughs where lovers swoon,
A squirrel searches for a boon.
Kissing with a peppermint twist,
While grandma's cookies vanish in mist!

Mistletoe hangs, what a sight,
Couples battle, laughter takes flight.
Yet one old lad with a cheeky grin,
Sneaks in for a kiss—oh, where's his kin?

The cat's in charge of the scene,
Chasing bows that gleam and preen.
A holiday dance, oh what a chance,
While everyone shimmies in their pants!

Wistful Wishes on Winter Breezes

Winds whisper tales of snowflakes shy,
As mittens wave a jolly goodbye.
Hot chocolate wishes in mugs so round,
While friendly dogs tumble on the ground.

Sledding down hills, laughter explodes,
Catching winter's joy on snowy roads.
Victory screams from lips so bright,
As snowballs fly like pure delight!

Chimneys puffing with smokey cheer,
Santa's sleigh is lingering near.
Oh, what a sight, the kids ask why,
Every day feels like a pie in the sky!

Glistening Trails of Holiday Joy

Lights twinkle like stars on parade,
While children giggle, their plans are made.
Tinsel cascades down from the tree,
As holiday spirits are wild and free.

Gifts piled high, like a mountain peak,
With wrapping paper that's far from sleek.
A cat on a box, thinking it's grand,
While dog eyes the treats, a clever plan!

Cookies vanish, a sugary plight,
Leaving crumbs in the warmth of the night.
As laughter dances through the air,
Holiday joy—beyond compare!

Memories of Comfort in a Cozy Nest

In a nest of pillows, so comfy and bright,
I sat with my snacks, late into the night.
The cat was my guardian, all fluffy and round,
While dreams of pizza danced in my found.

A blanket cocoon made me feel like a queen,
With crumbs on my shirt—I'm a fashionable scene!
The TV flickered, my favorite show played,
But I paused for popcorn—oh, what a trade!

Laughter bubbled up like my soda can's fizz,
As I reminisced what true comfort is.
Chasing memories now, my heart feels so light,
In this cozy nest, everything's just right!

So here's to the moments, sweet and absurd,
To quirky adventures that seem quite unheard.
Wrapped in my blanket, snug as a bug,
Life's silly comforts, I'll always hug.

The Harmony of Flickering Flames

In the hearth's warm glow, the marshmallows rise,
I sing like a bird, but it sounds like a … sigh.
The flames dance around, with a flicker and pop,
Oh no! There goes my hot dog; why can't they just stop?

With a s'more in my hand and my friends all a-grin,
We share ghost stories that make us spin.
But the shadows can scare, and the tales turn to fright,
Especially that one about the ghost in the night!

As sparklers twinkle, glitter light so divine,
We laugh at the sparks like they're sipping our wine.
The fire crackles, a music of sorts,
As we try to outwit each other with retorts.

From laughter to puns, the harmony flows,
The flames of our friendship, as bright as it glows.
So here's to the fire, the warmth, and the fun,
In the flickering flames, our hearts become one!

Enigmatic Elegance of the Snowy Night

The snowflakes are dancing, a chilly ballet,
In my puffy parka, I cheerfully sway.
The world is a canvas, so white and so bright,
And here I am, falling—oh! What a sight!

Snowmen are sculpted with glee and with flair,
I misplaced my carrot—was it whisked by the air?
The dogs run past dragging their owners in tow,
While I'm stuck frozen, just watching the show.

Yet mystery beckons in every snow drift,
A snowball flies forward—oh no! That's a gift!
With laughter and chaos, the playground is rife,
As I dodge every flake like I'm avoiding a knife.

But as evening descends on this magical night,
The stars peek out shyly, all twinkling and bright.
In the snowy embrace, the chill turns to cheer,
With joy in my heart, I'm thankful to be here!

Embracing the Chill with Open Hearts

The winter wind howls, it's a blustery day,
I bundled up tight just to bravely stray.
With mittens all mismatched and boots full of snow,
I tiptoe on ice like a one-legged crow.

Hot cocoa in hand, I warm up my toes,
As I savor each sip, the warm sweetness flows.
Ice skaters twirl like they're stuck in a dream,
But I can't balance, it's a comical theme.

With friends by my side, we gather and laugh,
Warming our spirits, forget the cold half.
We build a grand fort, oh, the laughter, it roars,
Until someone falls and flops on the floor!

So here's to the frost, and the chill in the air,
To laughter and joy shared with others, we care.
With hearts wide open, we'll conquer the freeze,
Embracing the cold, with laughter, we seize!

Melodies of the Whispering Pines

The pines play tunes that make you grin,
With squirrels dancing, let the fun begin.
A woodpecker's drum joins the groove,
Nature's band on this leafy move.

A rabbit hops with a tutu flair,
While owls hoot as if they don't care.
The sun peeks in, a spotlight bright,
Twirling trees make it quite a sight.

The breeze whispers jokes through the leaves,
As acorns roll like little thieves.
A chipmunk chirps a silly song,
Join the laughter, you can't go wrong.

So let's all sway to nature's beat,
With every stomp, we feel the heat.
The pines may whisper, the birds may sing,
But it's the giggles that make us swing.

Reviving Traditions with a Spark

Gather 'round for a quirky feast,
With Auntie's pie and Uncle's yeast.
Old recipes that make us cringe,
But we stir it up with a cheeky grin.

The kitchen's chaos, flour on the floor,
While Grandma's dance moves leave us wanting more.
We attempt her old-timey jig,
But end up looking like a sad twig.

Traditions tangled like grandma's yarn,
We laugh and shout, "This can't be born!"
Yet every flop brings us more cheer,
Reviving it all with love, never fear.

So here's to mishaps, let's toast and cheer,
With every failure, our bonds grow near.
In the kitchen chaos, we find our art,
Reviving traditions, straight from the heart.

The Wistful Dance of Enchanted Snows

Snowflakes twirl like ballerinas in flight,
As snowmen grin in the pale moonlight.
A sled goes zooming down a hill,
While kids yell 'Wheee!' with a snowy thrill.

Frosty fingers and noses red,
Hot cocoa laughs, and no one's fed.
The winter sun peeks, a laugh in disguise,
As mittens tango under cloudy skies.

But wait! What's that? A snowball fight,
Laughter echoes, oh what a sight!
A face full of snow, a giggly yelp,
Even the snowmen are laughing, they help.

So dance, dear friends, in the winter's glow,
With frosty friends we all know.
In this enchanted, snowy trance,
We'll giggle and wiggle, and take a chance.

A Wreath of Memories for the Present

Hanging laughter on an old oak door,
With ties of memories from yesteryear.
A wreath of joy made with love and cheer,
Each glimpse brings back a hearty tear.

Bright ribbons twist like tales retold,
Of family dinners and grandpa bold.
Every ornament's a story divine,
In laughter and warmth, memories shine.

With pinecones placed like jokes in disguise,
And mistletoe hung low with sneaky eyes.
We gather 'round, telling tales from the past,
With every chuckle, the shadows are cast.

So hang up your memories, laugh at the past,
Create new ones that'll always last.
In this wreath of joy, let love be our guide,
As we dance through the seasons, side by side.

Frosty Windows and Whirling Flakes

Frosty windows, what a sight,
Snowflakes dance in pure delight.
My cocoa's gone, oh what a shame,
Guess I'll sip this soup, not quite the same.

The snowman's head is way too round,
He borrowed my hat, but won't stick around.
Sledding down the hill like a rocket,
I swear, I landed in someone's pocket!

A snowball fight broke out today,
My friend's now frozen, what can I say?
Next time we'll use soft fluffy balls,
To spare the pain of icy calls.

With every flake I see a grin,
Winter's here, let the fun begin!
Frosty windows, let's not pout,
There's joy and laughter, there's no doubt.

A Canvas of Stars Over Hushed Streets

Stars are twinkling like a disco ball,
Over quiet streets where shadows crawl.
I tripped on my shoes, it's quite a feat,
Land on my face, let this night be sweet.

The moon's a friend, always glowing bright,
Casting silly shadows, what a sight!
I waved to a tree, it didn't wave back,
Guess it's busy plotting its own snack.

Whispers of neighbors, soft and low,
Sharing secrets with their stewardess crow.
"Hey, is that a dog or a furry hat?"
Oh wait, it's just a cat, fancy that!

Under blankets, I hide from the cold,
Counting all the stars, as I grow old.
In this canvas of night, I want to stay,
While my snacks keep calling, "Just one more tray!"

Whispers of Hope in the Chill

In the chill, whispers dance and play,
Hope's little spark keeps the gloom at bay.
Wrapped in layers, cozy and warm,
I dream of summer and forget the harm.

The wind outside is a mischievous friend,
Stealing hats and scarves, can it just pretend?
"Let it blow," I laugh, with a hearty cheer,
It can't mess with me, I'm snug right here!

Snowmen gossip, catch the latest news,
One's lost a carrot, feeling quite blue.
With every blink, a joke takes flight,
Even in winter, I'm feeling just right.

Whispers of hope and little grins,
Chasing away the winter's sins.
So let it snow; I'll laugh, not chill,
With every giggle, I've got a thrill.

Illuminated Nights of Tranquility

Lights are twinkling like a Christmas tree,
In a world that feels quite fancy-free.
I lost my shoe on the icy track,
Looks like I'll just have to head back!

Candlelight flickers, shadows sway,
Secretly plotting their dance away.
I joined in the fun, but tripped on the mat,
Now I'm the star, oh, imagine that!

With each warm mug, the night grows bright,
Sipping marshmallows 'til they take flight.
Around the table, laughter and cheer,
"Who ate the last bite?" Oh dear, oh dear!

So in these nights, when all seems still,
Let's toast to moments that give us a thrill.
Illuminated hearts, a cheerful crew,
Together in warmth, just me and you!

Narnia's Glow Beyond the Door

Beyond the wardrobe, a land so bright,
Where talking beasts take quirky flight.
The snow is deep, the fun is grand,
But I lost my socks in that magic land.

There's a lion who claims he's king of the beasts,
While Lucy snickers, munching on feasts.
Edmund's stuck with some Turkish delight,
Bet he'd trade it for a cozy night!

A witch in furs, with a frosty stare,
Sipping hot cocoa, what a peculiar affair!
With every adventure, my heart starts to race,
But who knew a wardrobe could lead to such space?

So here's to Narnia, a whimsy delight,
Where anything can happen, day or night.
I'll gladly return, though beware the snow,
It'll hide your socks—oh no, where did they go?

Memories Wrapped in Woolen Throws

On chilly nights, I snuggle tight,
With woolen throws, a pure delight.
Grandma's stories weave through the air,
Of mischievous cats, and a golden bear.

These blankets hold tales, a treasure chest,
Of knitters gone wild, who built quite the nest.
Each patch a memory, a giggle or frown,
Wrapped up so snug, like a fluffy gown.

We sit by the fire, sipping on tea,
A world full of laughter, just you and me.
But watch out for crumbs, when you take a bite,
The cats have their paws, they're ready to fight!

So here's to wool, our cozy embrace,
Turning cold moments to a warm space.
May every thread, with love it bestow,
Keep us wrapped tightly in memories' glow.

Lanterns Against the Winter's Dark

When winter falls, and shadows creep,
Lanterns twinkle, secrets to keep.
They dance in the night, flickering bright,
But I trip on the steps, what a sight!

Their glow leads the way through icy streets,
With each handy bump, my nose meets the fleets.
I wave to the snowmen, all dressed in style,
With carrots for noses and hats with a smile.

Candles and laughter fill up the air,
As we sip hot chocolate without a care.
Yet somehow, I spill some down my front,
Oh dear, that marshmallow is quite the blunt!

So here's to the lanterns that light up our hearts,
Facing the winter with all of its parts.
Let's dance in the glow, and share a jest,
For laughter and light are the very best.

Snowflakes Carrying Secret Wishes

Snowflakes drift down, a soft, gentle tease,
Each one unique, like a sneeze in the breeze!
They swirl and they twirl, a whimsical show,
But catch one too fast, and they'll say, "Oh no!"

With every flake, a wish takes flight,
To find my lost mittens, make winter feel right.
And what do I wish? To skate without fall,
But I wobble and slide, I don't skate at all!

A snowman appears, with a grin on his face,
Made of ice and snow, he's found his place.
He tells me, "Don't worry, we all can't glide,
Just enjoy the flurries and take it in stride."

So here's to snowflakes, wishes on air,
Whimsies that fall like soft, frosty hair.
Let's laugh at the cold, raise cups full of cheer,
For through all this frost, friendship draws near!

Chilling Beauty in Glistening White

The snowflakes dance and twirl so bright,
Making snowmen laugh with pure delight.
But when I slip and land with a thud,
I question why I didn't wear my studs.

The icicles hang like frozen spears,
Reminding me of my chocolate fears.
As I munch on treats, the dogs will stare,
Wishing they too could join the fair.

With mittens on, I wave to the sky,
I see the clouds and wonder, why?
They're heavy with snow, and I'm here to say,
At least they didn't fall in my parfait!

Chilling beauty, a sight divine,
Until I slip on ice, oh, what a sign!
I greet the snow with a goofy dance,
While my backside's freezing in winter's chance.

Glowing Embers and Starry Skies

The fire crackles with a warming cheer,
As marshmallows roast, I shed a tear.
For every burnt treat, my heart does ache,
But gooey s'mores are worth the mistake!

The stars above twinkle like grand prix,
While I scan the sky for some light glee.
But all I spot are the planes on high,
Guess my wishes will just fly by!

Wrapped in blankets, cozy and snug,
Suddenly warm as I hug my mug.
But then I spill it, oh what a show,
The blanket now drenched, what a low blow!

Glowing embers, a cracking song,
As I hum to tunes that just feel wrong.
Yet laughter fills the chilly night air,
Just me, the fire, and trials to share.

The Language of Snowflakes

Each snowflake whispers secrets pure,
Like tiny cryptics—to decode, I'm sure.
But they melt so fast, what's the use,
I guess they just want to cut me loose!

While children catch flakes upon their tongues,
I stand amazed, my trepidation stung.
The whiteness falls like nature's confetti,
Yet I'm here sneezing, feeling unsteady!

A snowflake lands on my nose so cute,
I try to say hello—but can't, it's fruit!
A gentle drip leads to an icy face,
Thank you, snowflake, for the cold embrace!

So let it fall, the winter's decree,
In this frozen language, I'll just be me.
Each flake a giggle, soft as a sigh,
I'll dance in the snow, until I'm dry!

Envelopes of Warmth in Frigid Times

Wrapped like a burrito, I sit in delight,
Hot chocolate's steaming, oh what a sight.
But when I take a sip, it upends my plan,
The cocoa goes dribble—just like my tan!

Wrapped in layers, I waddle about,
Like a fluffy penguin, there's no doubt.
But then I trip, my own two left feet,
And my hot cocoa lands at my seat!

Scarves wrapped so tight, they block my view,
I can't see the snow, or walk straight too.
It's a game of chess with my own feet,
As mittens wave hello to my defeat!

But in frigid times, there's joy to find,
With laughter and warmth, I'm always kind.
So here's to the mishaps, the cocoa spills,
In this winter wonderland, let's chase those thrills!

Whispers Between Twinkling Trees

The trees gossip softly at night,
Their leaves making quite the uproar,
One says, "Did you see that owl?"
The other giggles, "He's quite the bore!"

They chuckle loud as stars blink bright,
With rustling tales of squirrels and nuts,
A raccoon sneaks in, thinking he's slick,
But the trees sigh, "Oh, here come the ruts!"

The moon joins in, it's quite a scene,
With moonbeams poring over the grounds,
"Oh, look! That cat thinks he can dance!"
The woods erupt with hoots and sounds!

As dawn tiptoes, they hush their cheer,
"See you tonight, when the gossip rolls!"
But the trees know, with wisdom near,
That all their ramblings brighten souls!

A Cascade of Winter's Radiance

Winter's here with frosty glee,
Snowflakes dance, oh can't you see!
They twirl like ballerinas bold,
While hot cocoa warms hands like gold.

The snowman's got a carrot nose,
But it's floppy and often dozes.
Kids giggle as he starts to sway,
"Hey, Mr. Snowman, come out and play!"

A snowball whizzes, oh what a blast,
But somehow, it hits the dog at last!
He shakes and rolls, then joins the fun,
Barking "Snowball fights? Now that's well done!"

The winter sun smiles wide and bright,
As shadows race in pure delight.
So let's make snow forts, cheer loud and clear,
In this winter wonder, there's joy to revere!

Carols Carried by the Wind

The wind sings low, a cheeky tune,
While leaves join in, wishing for June.
A squirrel's caught, mid-rap, it's true,
Dropping his acorns, just for a view!

Birds chime in with a feathery flair,
"Hey, how 'bout sharing that juicy pear?"
All join hands (well, wings, of course),
Creating a choir with mighty force!

The breeze plays tricks, oh what a tease,
Wiggles your hat off just to please.
"Catch it quick!" your friends all shout,
But laughter's louder as they flake out!

So let's sing carols, loud and clear,
Join the bonkers wind without fear.
In the merry gusts of holiday cheer,
Life's a raucous party, never drear!

The Allure of Snow-Blanketed Fields

Snow blankets fields like fluffy beds,
While rabbits hop with snowball heads.
They seem to plan a bouncy race,
But trip and roll, oh what a face!

The snow's so deep, it swallows shoes,
Chasing dogs, it gives a snooze.
"What's that?" they bark, and leap in glee,
Finding a glimmering snow-dream spree!

The icicles drip from winter's crown,
Turning the landscape into a gown.
They shimmer and shine, a crystal carnival,
But care for your head, it can be terrible!

As the sun dips low, the colors spread,
While kids frolic, necks and noses red.
In fields of white, with laughter we yield,
Joy reigns supreme on this snowy field!

Soft Footfalls on a Winter Path

With every step, a crunching sound,
A symphony of winter found.
My boots are clumsy, oh what fun,
Keeping me upright is half the run.

The snowflakes whirl, a dance of cold,
Each breath a puff, like tales of old.
I slip and slide, a frosty ballet,
Shuffling with flair, in my own way.

A snowman's grin, it's wide and bright,
His carrot nose, not quite in sight.
He tips his hat, says, 'Join the dance!'
But I just smile and take a chance.

So here I go, my winter waltz,
With gleeful giggles in winter's vaults.
Soft footfalls lead to laughter's spark,
In snowy realms, I leave my mark.

Hearth and Home Wrapped in Peace

The fire's crackle, a cozy glow,
Wraps the room in warmth, you know.
I sip my cocoa, marshmallows afloat,
While visions of cookies dance and gloat.

The cat's on the rug, a ball of fluff,
Pretending he's tough, but that's quite rough.
He dreams of mice and daring feats,
While I just enjoy my warm winter treats.

Outside the wind howls, a whimpering sound,
But with cookies and comfort, joy's abound.
My socks mismatched, a colorful sight,
Inside my fortress, I'll stay all night.

So here I nest, with blankets galore,
Hearth and home, who could ask for more?
A peaceful evening, all snug and tight,
In my cozy corner, it feels just right.

The Enchantment of a Gentle Snowfall

Oh look, the snowflakes float and swirl,
Like little dancers in a twirling whirl.
They tiptoe down, so light, so fair,
But on my nose? They get stuck there!

They settle softly on every tree,
A snowy cloak for all to see.
But watch your step, it's slippery ground,
One wrong move, and you'll spin around!

The kid in the sled is flying fast,
Squeals of laughter, oh what a blast!
But he hits a bump, the sled takes flight,
Now he's a snowball, a comical sight!

So when the snow falls, don't hold back,
Join the fun, embrace the lack.
For every flake brings joy anew,
And creates a dance for me and you.

Dreams Danced Upon Frosted Grounds

Upon the frost, my thoughts take flight,
In visions grand, both merry and bright.
I dream of snowmen with top hats tall,
And penguins that waddle, having a ball.

In winter's grip, the trees are bare,
But my mind wanders, without a care.
I'd build a castle, all made of ice,
With frosty turrets, oh so nice!

The moon grins down, a curious spy,
As snowflakes twinkle in the night sky.
I'll waltz with shadows, skimming the ground,
On frosted tips, my joy unbound.

So let the winter's chill knock at my door,
I'll dance with dreams and ask for more.
For every crunch beneath my feet,
Is a melody sweet, an adventure neat!

Radiant Shadows through the Frost

In the morning light we glide,
With pinky toes that slip and slide.
Snowflakes dance on noses bright,
As we laugh, a frosty sight.

Radiant shadows, wild and free,
Creating art on you and me.
Frosty winks and icy grins,
Winter's joy, where fun begins.

Mittens on, but fingers peek,
To grab the snowballs that we seek.
A slippery chase, a joyful race,
With giggles echoing through the space.

So let's embrace this chilly cheer,
With jumpy hops and hearty beer.
Radiant shadows, laugh out loud,
In frosty fun, we're feeling proud.

Frosted Breath and Heartfelt Hugs

Frosted breath upon the air,
Our cheeks are red, we hardly care.
Wrapped in layers, it's snuggle time,
With cocoa mugs that feel sublime.

Heartfelt hugs and silly glee,
Warmth that pours as we all flee.
Snowmen laugh, their noses bright,
Made of carrots and pure delight.

Slipping here and tumbling there,
With flailing arms, we try to bear.
A snowy hill, our sleds will fly,
With squeals and shouts like birds on high.

Frosty kisses, winter's spark,
Even the penguins join our lark.
So gather round, let laughter sing,
In frosted breath, our hearts take wing.

Dreams Wrapped in Silver and Gold

In dreams so bright, silver and gold,
Frosted visions, stories untold.
Snowflakes whisper, secrets to share,
As we twirl in winter's care.

Petty worries tossed aside,
We embrace the chill, with hearts open wide.
Laughter sparkles in icy streams,
Filling our world with whimsical dreams.

With twinkling lights on trees that sway,
Winter's magic in full display.
Hot cocoa spills in a frothy mess,
Wrapped up snug, we'll never guess.

Dreams painted on a frosted pane,
Merry moments, let joy reign.
For this season, let's not be old,
We'll dance in dreams wrapped in silver and gold.

Celestial Chimes and Frosty Air

In frosty air, the bell chimes ring,
Ding-dong merrily, let joy spring.
Snowflakes fall with a gentle cheer,
As we make wishes to share this year.

Celestial vibes float soft and light,
Sparkling stars winking through the night.
Hot waffles stack high, syrupy bliss,
Each bite's a giggle, we can't miss.

Footprints squish in the thick white fluff,
A frosty adventure, just pure luck.
With grumpy cats in knitted hats,
They join our fun, but refuse to chat.

So take a breath of the frosty air,
And spread our laughter everywhere.
In celestial chimes and laughter's loop,
We dance in winter's joyful scoop.

Luminous Dreams on Crisp Nights

The stars are winking, oh so bright,
A squirrel in a jacket, ready for flight.
Hot cocoa spills, oh what a scene,
Was that a snowman? Or just a caffeine machine?

The moon is giggling, can't you see?
I swear it just winked at me.
Frosty breath dances in the air,
Hoping my hat doesn't too, beware!

Snowflakes flutter like tiny sprites,
Each one cheerfully landing in fights.
A snowball whizzes, misses its mark,
Just like my aim when it's after dark!

In dreams I ride a shimmering sleigh,
With penguins directing, leading the way.
Oh what fun on this merry night,
Luminous laughter until first light!

The Magic of Winter's Embrace

Bundled up tight, I stroll down the lane,
My nose is red, but I feel no pain.
Chasing my shadow, a clumsy ballet,
Is it snow, or did they just sprinkle confetti today?

Hot soup in hand, it drips on my chin,
A taste of winter - where do I begin?
Snowflakes that tickle as they fall down,
I giggle and wobble, my best winter frown.

Icicles hang, they shimmer and sway,
A frosty Picasso, nature's own play.
Watch out for goblins lurking inside,
Turns out they're just kids, playing with pride!

Every day's magic, who knew it was here?
With tales of penguins and snowman fear.
In every flake lies a spark of delight,
Winter's embrace is a pure silly sight!

A Glistening Tapestry of Joy

Glittering snowflakes blanket the ground,
Happiness sprinkles in joy all around.
Frosty the snowman, with buttons of coal,
He's got more style than a penguin in a troll!

Children laugh, they tumble and roll,
Snowballs flying like a playful patrol.
Sleds zoom past, a racetrack of glee,
Watch out! Here comes a snowball cannon, whee!

The hot cider bubbles, the marshmallows float,
And a leaping deer just stole my coat.
Winter's a playground full of pure cheer,
With laughter that rings through the whole hemisphere!

A tapestry woven of moments so bright,
Where every cold day feels cozy and right.
In laughter and snowflakes, we find our way,
A glistening joy for each winter's day!

Hushed Carols in the Moonlight

Under the stars, we croon and sway,
Hushed carols echo in a frosty ballet.
The moon joins in, it starts to glow,
In a jolly duet, we steal the show!

Icicles drip, like a metronome's beat,
While reindeer tap dance in snow-covered feet.
Frosty swings his arms in delight,
As we sing carols all through the night.

With every note, the chill feels warm,
As laughter and music create a charm.
Even the owls are dancing along,
In the hush of winter, we all belong!

So gather 'round for a night full of cheer,
Where every heart feels joy when it's here.
With hushed carols in the shimmering light,
Winter's our stage, oh what a sight!

Enchanted Evening of Shining Dreams

In a forest of giggles, owls wear hats,
Squirrels throwing parties, dancing on mats.
The stars laugh so loud, they should be banned,
As unicorns prance with a soda in hand.

Fairies trade whispers for bedtime jokes,
While gnomes are caught telling puns to the folks.
Witches brew laughter in bubbling potions,
Creating wild storms of magical notions.

A dragon does salsa, flaming tail in the air,
The moon joins the fun, with a clap and a stare.
In this enchanted realm, no worries reside,
Just the joy of the night, on a whimsical ride.

So come take a peek, shed your mundane schemes,
Join the parade of this night filled with dreams.
With laughter as currency, let worries take flight,
In this enchanted evening, everything's right!

The Stillness of a Winter's Twilight

Snowflakes are sneezing, they fall with a twirl,
Trees wear white blankets, like a frosty girl.
The cold air is thick with a crispy delight,
While penguins in bowties prepare for a fight.

Chilly winds whisper, 'Just get out of bed!'
But cozy socks hug toes, in a slumber ahead.
Mittens on snails who ride slowly and sly,
As squirrels wear their scarves and complain with a sigh.

Icicles dangle like teeth from above,
While snowmen declare they're created with love.
Yet, one little snowman dreams of a tan,
He wonders how summer would suit a snowman.

When dusk settles softly, the world takes a pause,
As laughter erupts from the trees and the cause.
In this stillness of twilight, peace warms the cold,
With each snowy giggle, a story unfolds.

Frosted Echoes of Love and Light

In a land of frost, where the pine trees snicker,
Lovers share cocoa, and the marshmallows flicker.
Hearts bounce like snowballs, creamy and sweet,
While giggles of love fill the air with a beat.

Icicles whisper soft, sweet nothings on eaves,
And starlight's shy dance tugs at our sleeves.
Cupid's caught sneezing, his bow's on the fritz,
As hearts form in snow, he just can't take hits.

With frosted echoes that twirl in delight,
Each glance is a melody, soft as the night.
Love wraps round us, like the glow of a fire,
In this sweet winter wonder, our hearts never tire.

So let's toast with mugs, in this frosty embrace,
And dance with the echoes of love's gentle grace.
In a world full of laughter, and joy shining bright,
Here's to frosted echoes of love and light!

Moonlit Reflections on Soft Snow

Under the moon's gaze, bears waltz and they sway,
While rabbits compose symphonies night and day.
The snow glitters softly, like diamonds on lace,
As the stars join the party, keeping up the pace.

A chilly trombone plays a jazzy old tune,
As raccoons in tuxedos break dance by the moon.
Penguins are juggling fish, all slippery and slick,
While snowflakes fall softly, like magic, and quick.

In the meadow of giggles, a snow angel grins,
Counting misplaced snowballs, oh how time spins!
With laughter galore, the night's filled with cheer,
As the moon winks at snowmen, standing so near.

So dance on the snow with your wonderful friends,
With moonlit reflections, the joy never ends.
In this soft snowy wonder, let the good times flow,
As we twirl and we laugh in the shimmer of snow.

A Hearth's Embrace

The fire crackles, embers dance,
My socks are warm, my drink's in France.
The cat steals my seat, oh what a sin,
With all this warmth, who needs to win?

The marshmallows melt, the cocoa's sweet,
I spill it again, it's a messy feat.
The log rolls over, gives me a grin,
I laugh so hard, my belly's chagrin.

A blanket fort rises, a castle grand,
With pillows and snacks, oh isn't it planned?
But who guards the snacks? The dog, I suppose,
He feigns innocence, the little doze.

Outside the snow falls, quiet and light,
While inside I'm wedged, in crackling delight.
So here's to the hearth, warm and affable,
A fluffy retreat, my home's most laughable.

Shimmering Nights of Solstice Glow

The stars are twinkling, dressed up bright,
I stumble outdoors, it's quite a sight.
My neighbors' lights blink, a disco ball,
I trip on the sidewalk, oh no, I fall!

The snowflakes tumble, making me freeze,
While I dream of beaches and salty breeze.
In my winter garb, I waddle around,
With mittens so big, they drag on the ground.

The solstice fest comes with treats galore,
But with my luck, I find none in store.
A cookie I spot, a snatched little bite,
But it crumbles to dust, oh what a plight!

Yet laughter rings through the frosted night,
As friends gather 'round, and spirits feel light.
For in this shimmer, with snowflakes that glow,
We find joy in laughter, through all of the snow.

Stars Wrapped in Snow

Bright stars above, like sprinkles on cake,
I gaze at the sky, but my back starts to ache.
The snowflakes whisper their cold little song,
While I dream of summer where I should belong.

Each flake is unique, like my socks with holes,
They dance in the breeze, like a group of moles.
I catch one on my tongue, what a sight to see,
But it melts too quickly, oh, woe is me!

Bright bundles of snow, like marshmallows too,
I challenge my friends to a snowball or two.
But alas, I slip, and I tumble, oh no!
The stars keep on laughing, as down I go low.

Yet laughter erupts, like fireworks bright,
Wrapping up snowballs with sheer delight.
So here I will stay, under stars all aglow,
In this frozen wonder, where giggles can grow.

The Silence of Candlelight

In candlelit rooms where shadows prance,
The wax drips slow, a delicate dance.
I light up a match, but it shatters my peace,
When the smoke sets off alarms, oh, good grief, cease!

With whispers of flame, the night seems to hum,
But the cat's in the corner, looks quite glum.
I reach for some chips, "What a terrible snack!"
But I spill the salsa, now I'm under attack!

With flickering lights, and a glass of red wine,
I ponder the world, lost in thought divine.
The cat gives me looks, as if to impart,
"Shall we have a dance? Get up and take part!"

So here in the silence, we sway to the beat,
With candlelight flickering, and a rhythm so sweet.
In the calm of the night, with giggles anew,
Together we twirl; the cat leads the crew.

Crystalline Portraits of Night's Peace

Underneath the moon's bright gaze,
The owls hoot in a quirky phase.
Stars drop by for a nighttime chat,
While cats assume their royal mat.

Snowflakes dance like they're in a show,
Each landing spot a hidden glow.
The world wrapped in a silvery cloak,
Where even the trees begin to joke.

Gentle whispers of the winter breeze,
Carry tales of squirrels, if you please.
They stash their acorns, what a sight!
Plotting snacks for their midnight bite.

So here we sit, hot cocoa in hand,
Watching the night's comedian stand.
Laughter wrapped in a frosty sheet,
Nature's punchlines can't be beat!

Hearts Alight with Winter's Glow

Frosty windows, a cozy sight,
While kids build snowmen with delight.
Snowballs fly with giggles so loud,
As parents sip cocoa, feeling proud.

Scarves wrapped tight, a fashionable trend,
Each breath puffing like a snowflake friend.
Shovels out for the great snow fight,
Oh, winter days are pure delight!

The fireplace crackles with warmth and cheer,
As stories unfold, bringing us near.
Each tale a tapestry, woven in streets,
Where laughter and memories are festive treats.

So gather round, let the fun unfurl,
In hearts alight, the winter's twirl.
With joy as our guide, we spring into play,
Chasing shivers of cold far away!

A Chronicle of Lights and Shadows

The streetlamps flicker a jaunty tune,
As shadows dance beneath the moon.
A cat with flair prances on by,
While lost socks squeak a confused sigh.

In alleys where echoes seem to play,
A pizza rat steals the night away.
Each corner hides a secret laugh,
As shadows draft a nightly photograph.

The stars debate their shining style,
One claims to outshine, but not for a while.
While lights compete in a glitter race,
Even shadows find their own embrace.

So raise a glass to the night's parade,
Where moments of joy and laughter are made.
In this quirky play of light's embrace,
Find solace in each shadowy space!

The Frosted Canvas of Twilight

As day slips off with a frosty sigh,
The sun dips low, bids goodbye.
Twilight brushes the sky with flair,
Transforming colors everywhere.

A penguin waddles in fashion quest,
Dressed in winter's finest vest.
While snowflakes twirl like tiny stars,
In comedic dance beneath Mars.

The twilight giggles, pinches the day,
Rabbits hop by in a playful ballet.
Stockings hung with hopes and dreams,
With candy canes, or so it seems.

So let the canvas paint our hearts,
With frosted smiles and silly parts.
In this joyful, frosty delight,
We cherish the warmth of winter's night!